ceiling fan

electric typewriter

blender

1

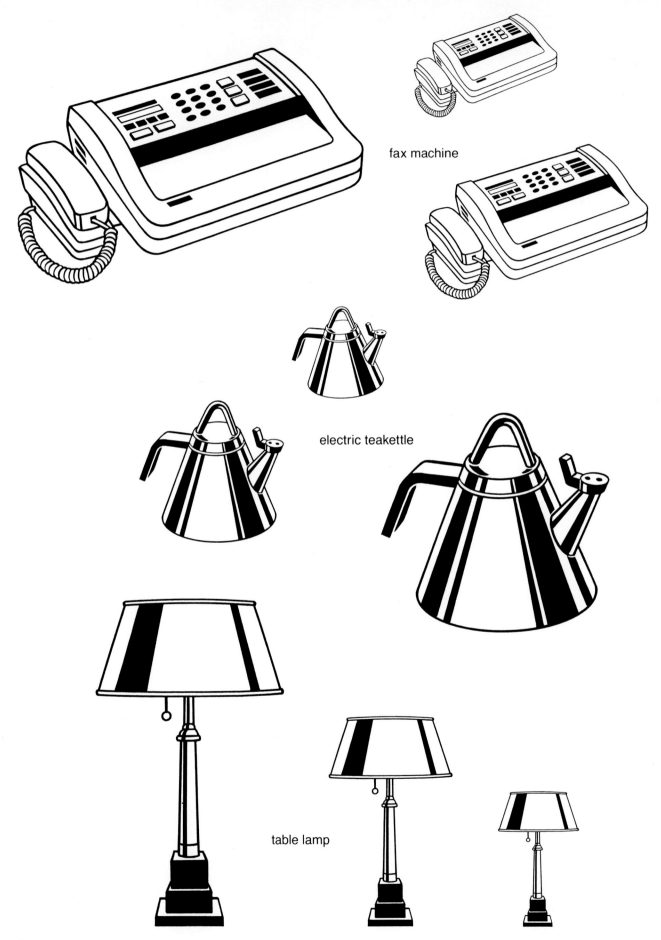

fax machine

electric teakettle

table lamp

drink mixer

wall telephone

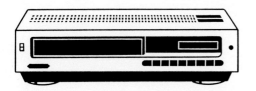

video cassette recorder

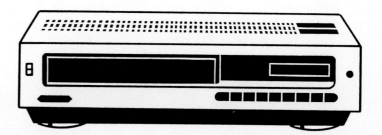

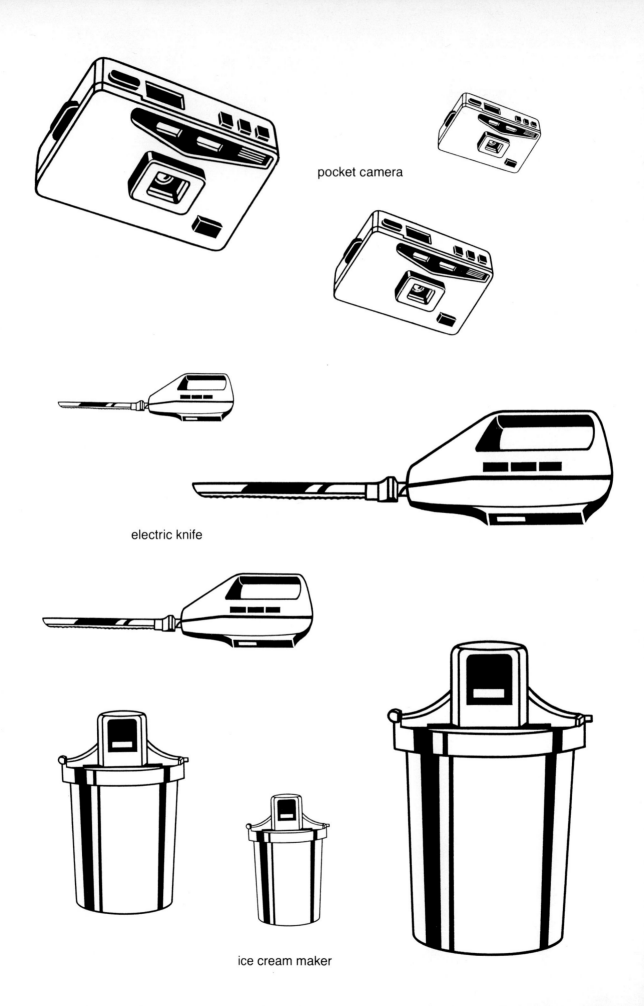

pocket camera

electric knife

ice cream maker

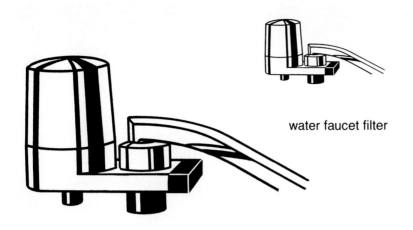
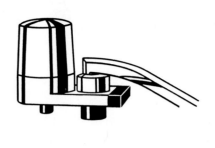

water faucet filter

stove

lawn mower

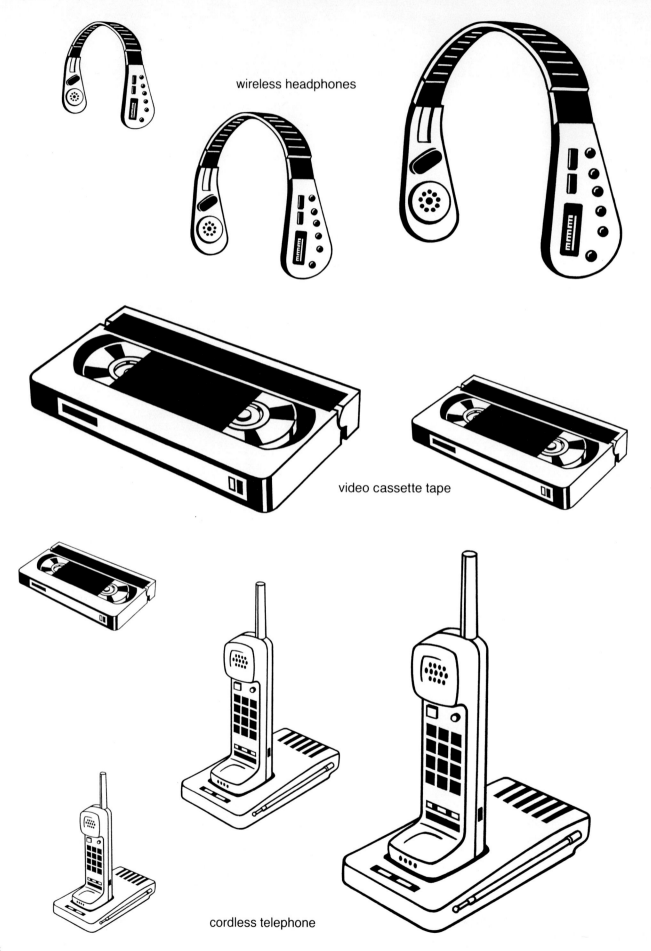

wireless headphones

video cassette tape

cordless telephone

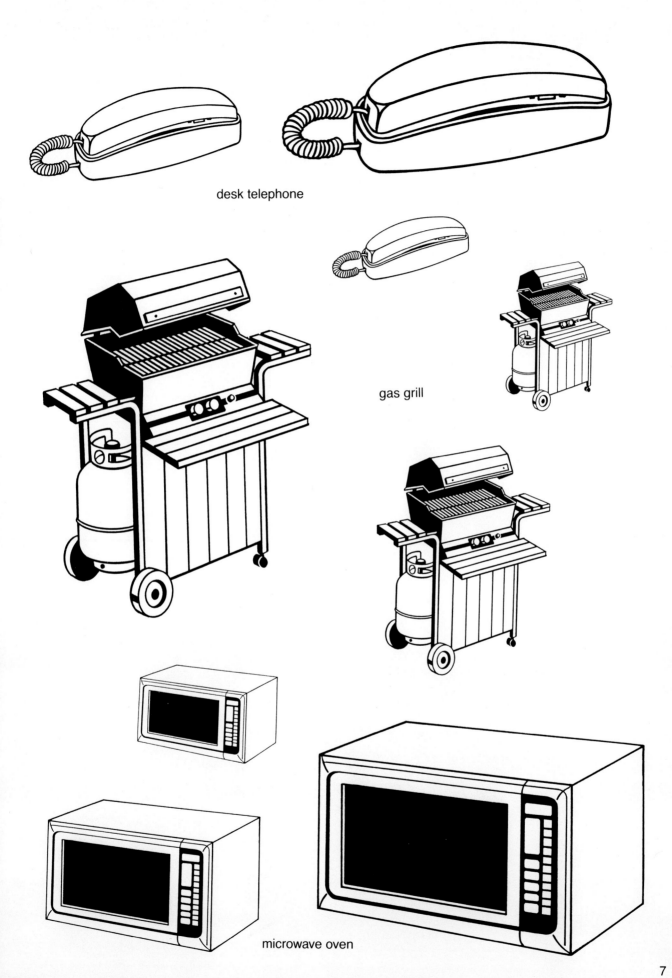

desk telephone

gas grill

microwave oven

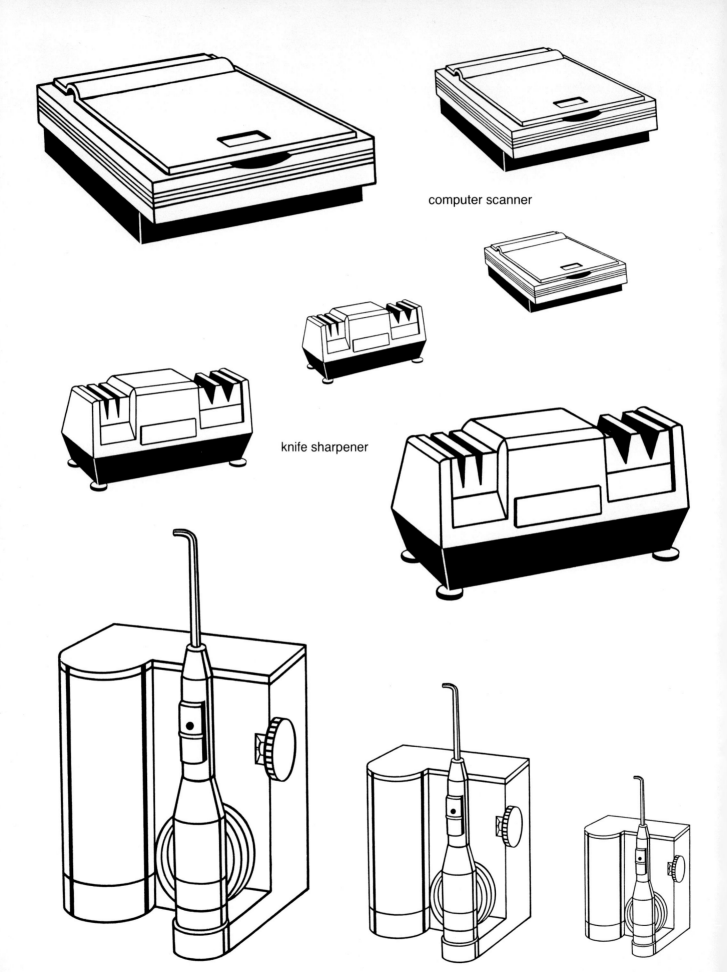

computer scanner

knife sharpener

electric dental hygiene system

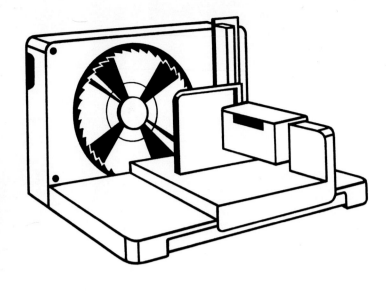
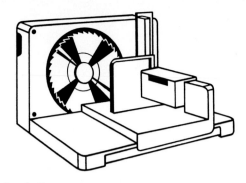

food slicer

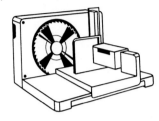

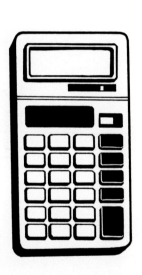

calculator

electric coffee grinder

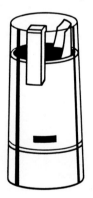

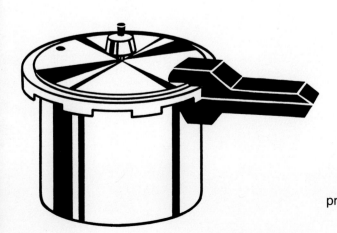

pressure cooker

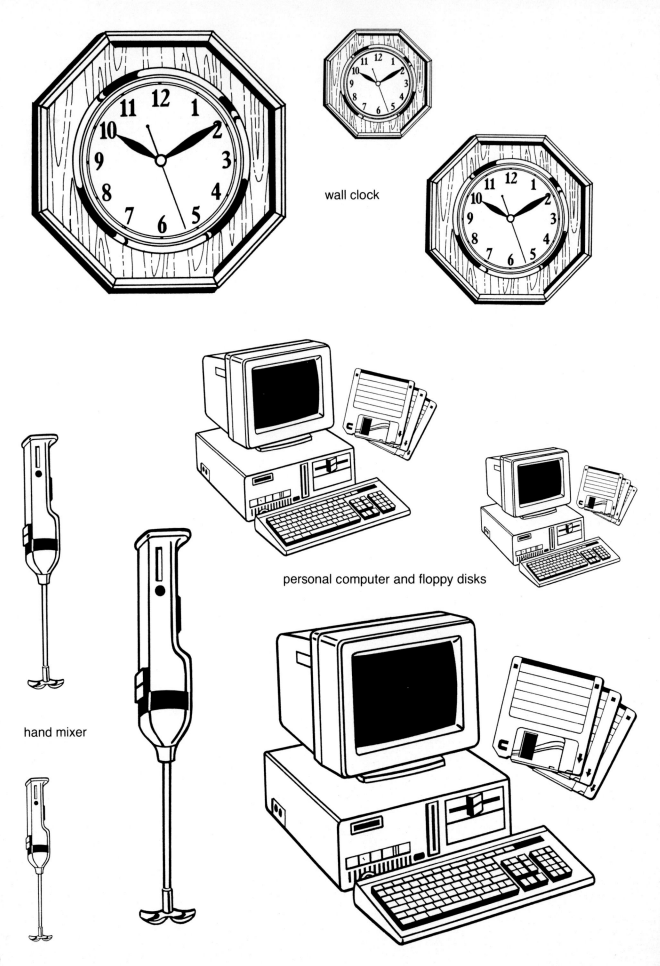

wall clock

personal computer and floppy disks

hand mixer

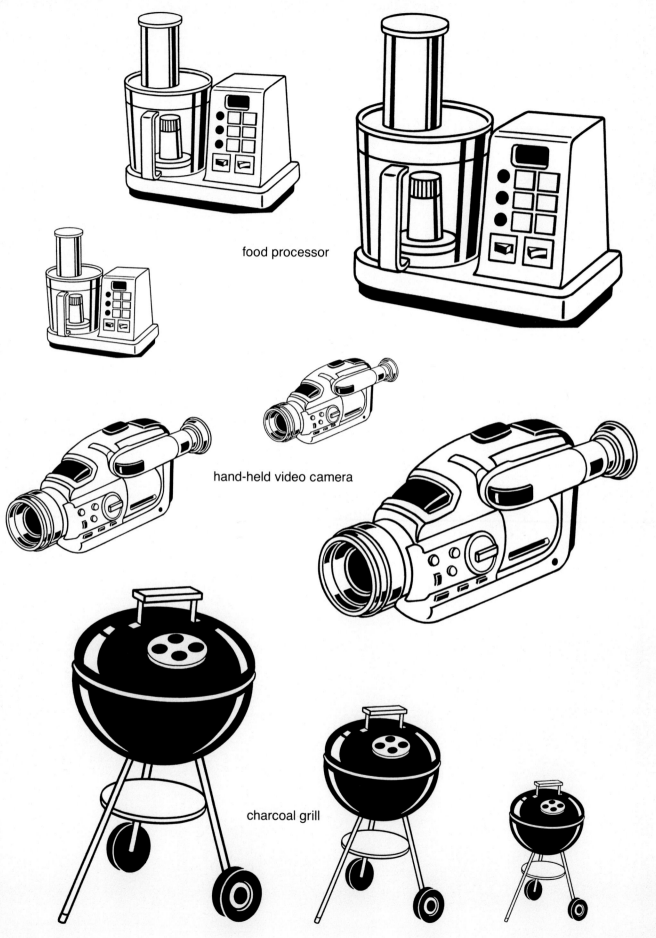

food processor

hand-held video camera

charcoal grill

electric fan

dryer

hand-held mixer

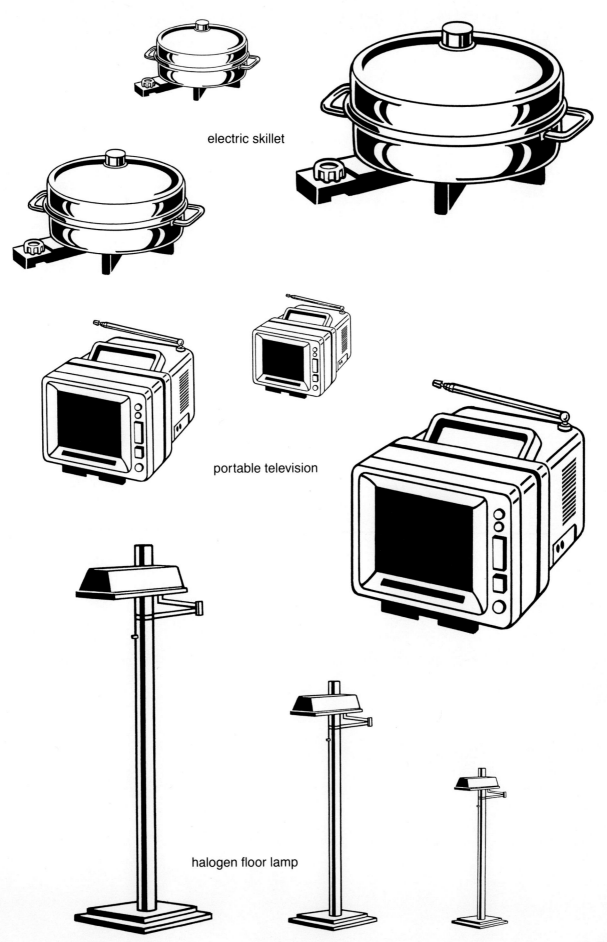

electric skillet

portable television

halogen floor lamp

alarm clock

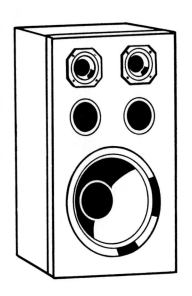
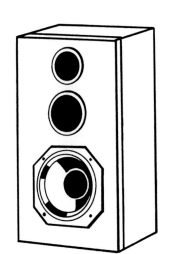
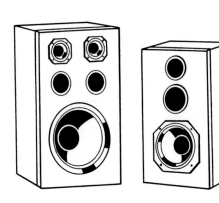
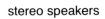

stereo speakers

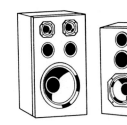

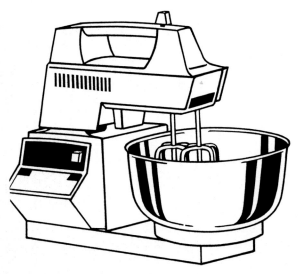

mixer

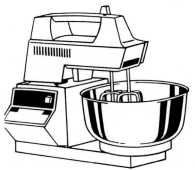

floppy disks

kitchen scale

electric shears

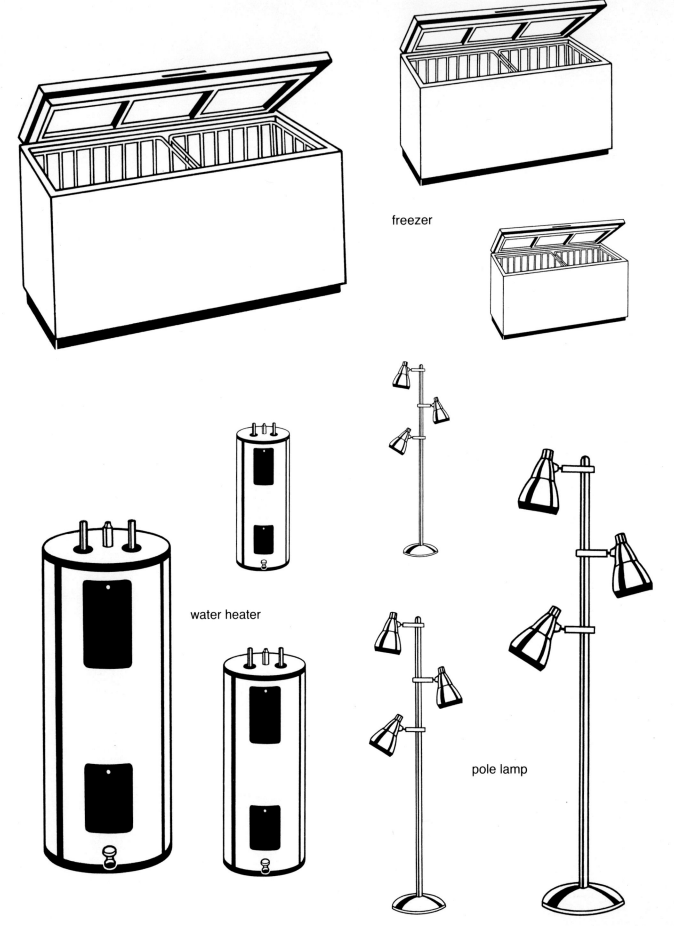

freezer

water heater

pole lamp

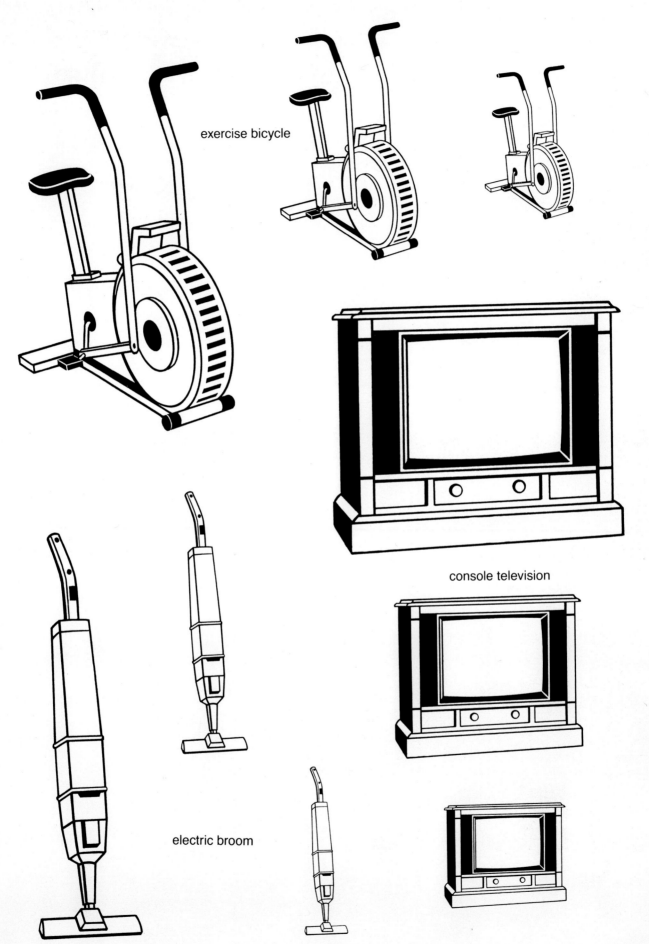

exercise bicycle

console television

electric broom

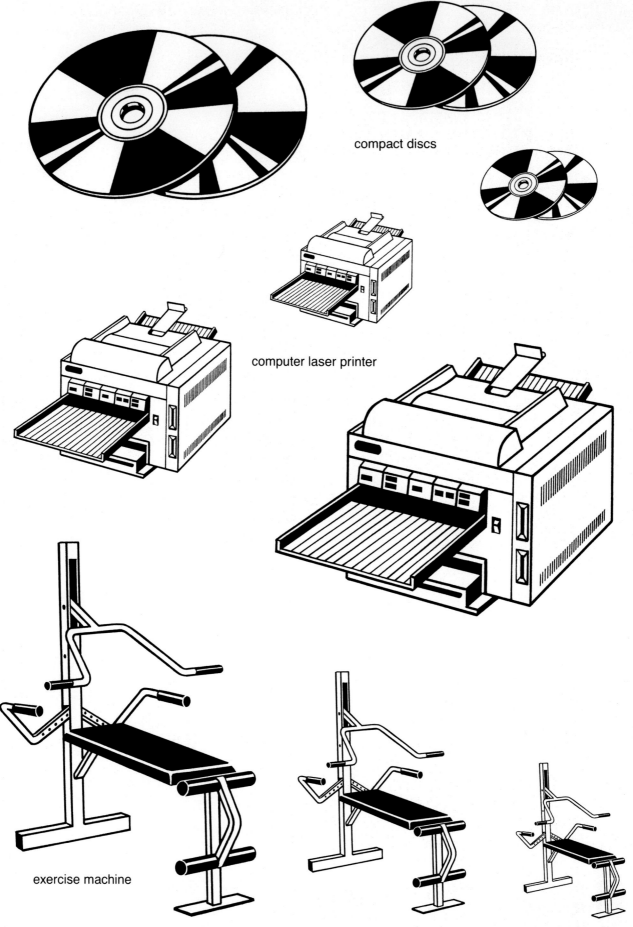

compact discs

computer laser printer

exercise machine

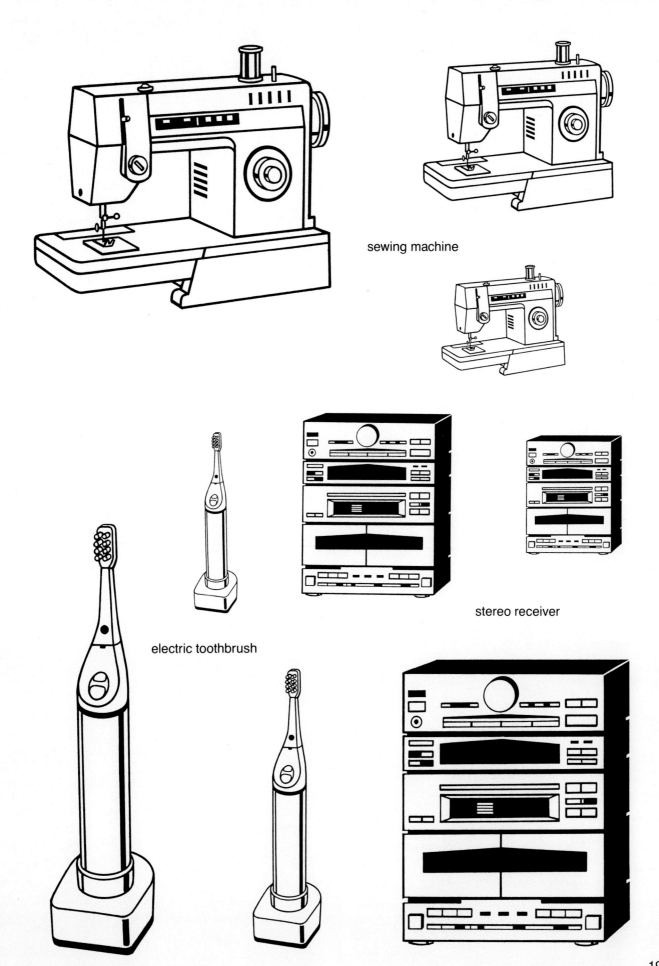

sewing machine

electric toothbrush

stereo receiver

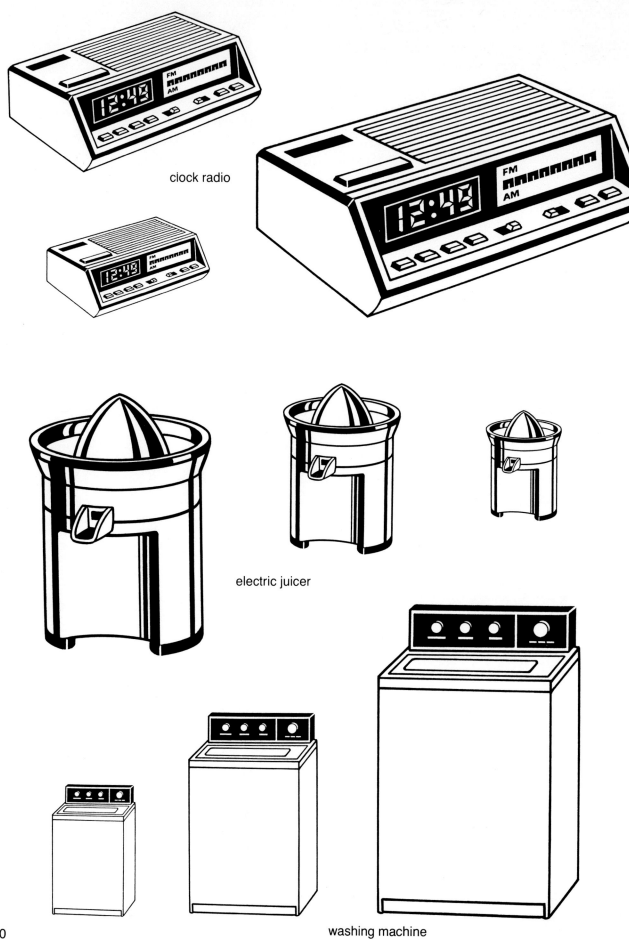

clock radio

electric juicer

washing machine

20

humidifier

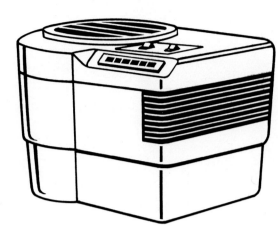

drip coffee maker

electric hedge trimmer

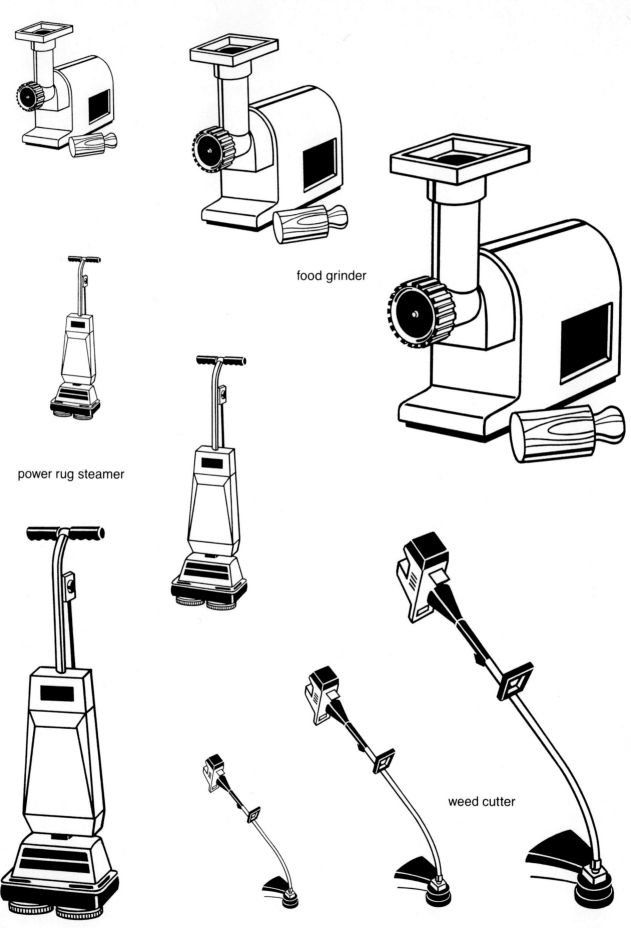

food grinder

power rug steamer

weed cutter

22

35mm camera

waffle iron

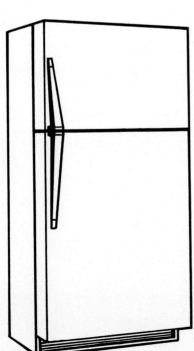

refrigerator

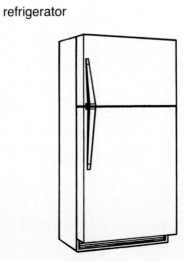

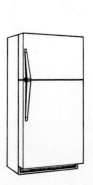

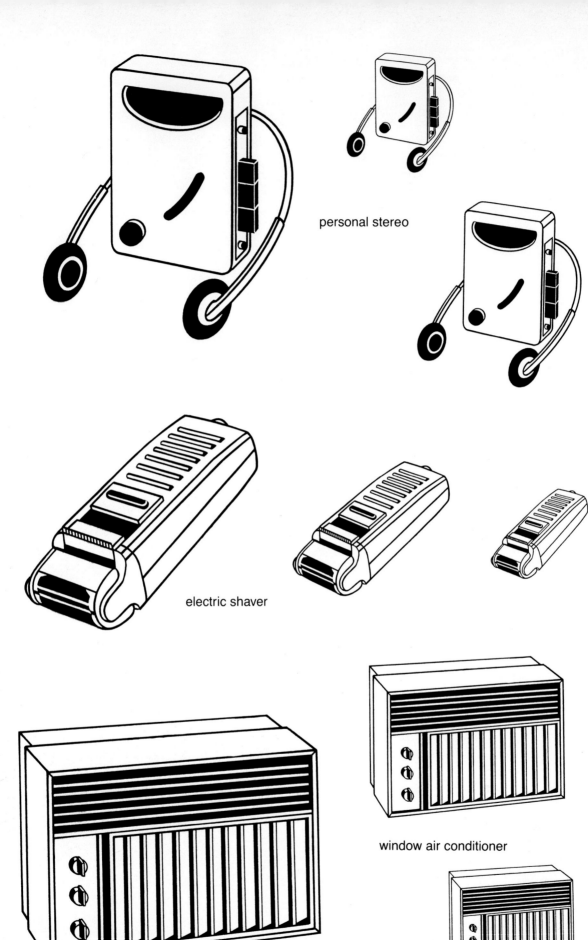

personal stereo

electric shaver

window air conditioner

coffee percolator

portable stereo

dishwasher

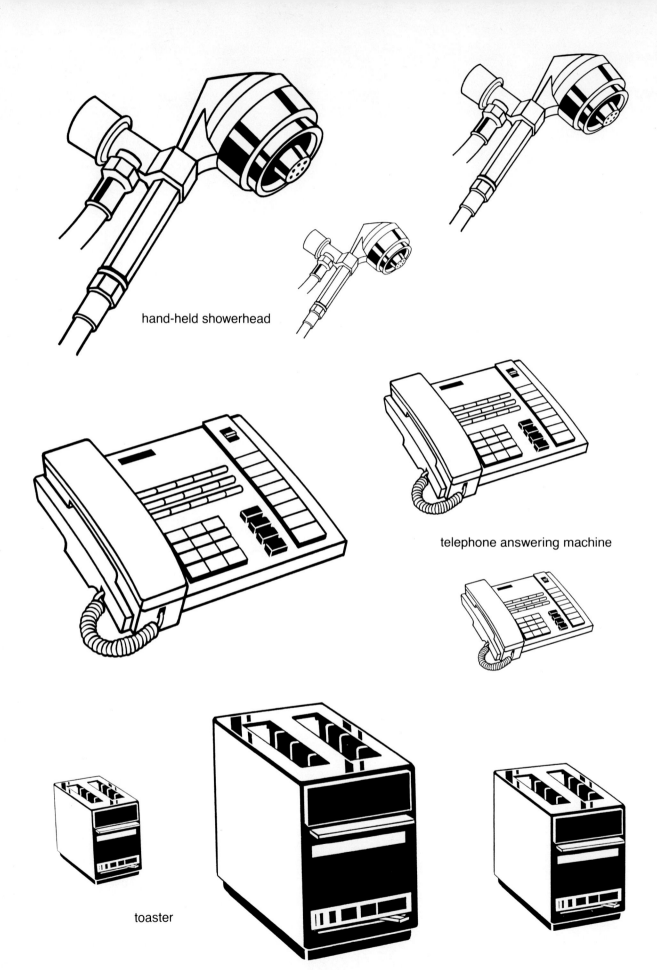

hand-held showerhead

telephone answering machine

toaster

blow dryer

electric pencil sharpener

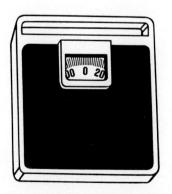

bathroom scale

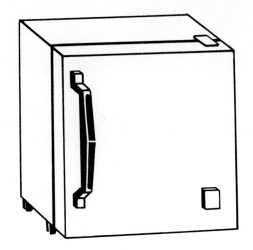

small refrigerator

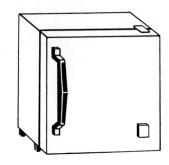

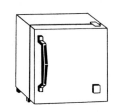

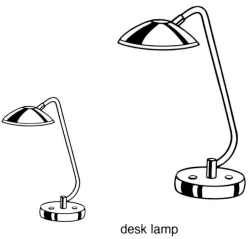

desk lamp

space heater

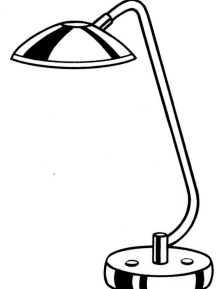

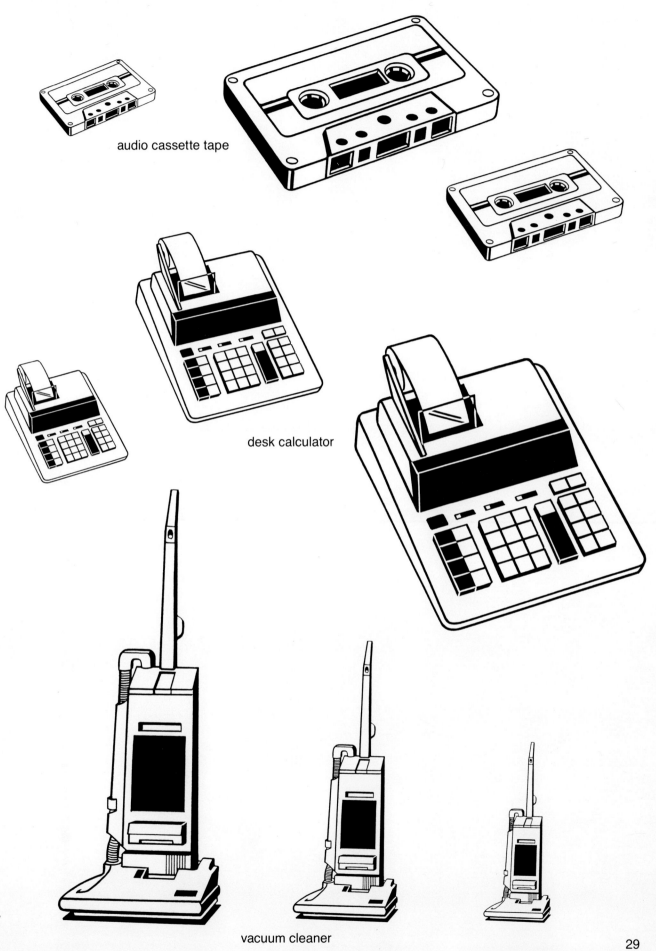

audio cassette tape

desk calculator

vacuum cleaner

29

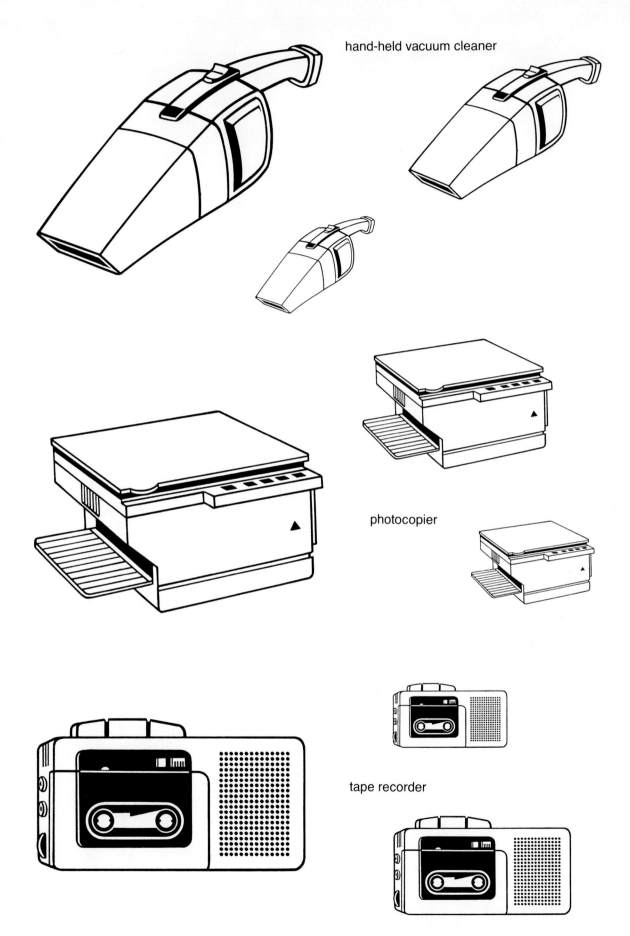

hand-held vacuum cleaner

photocopier

tape recorder

30

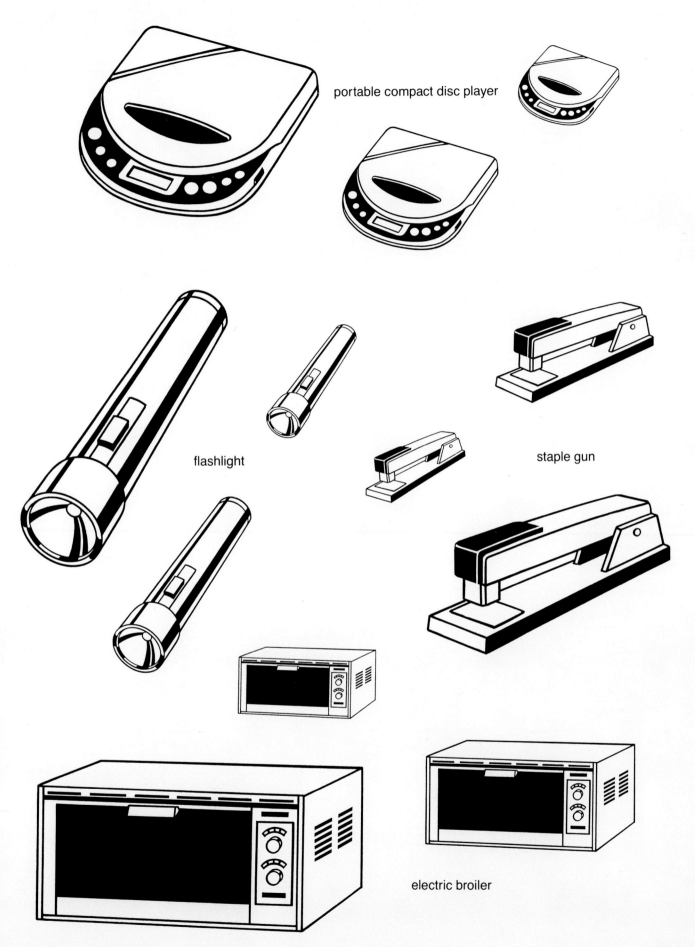

portable compact disc player

flashlight

staple gun

electric broiler

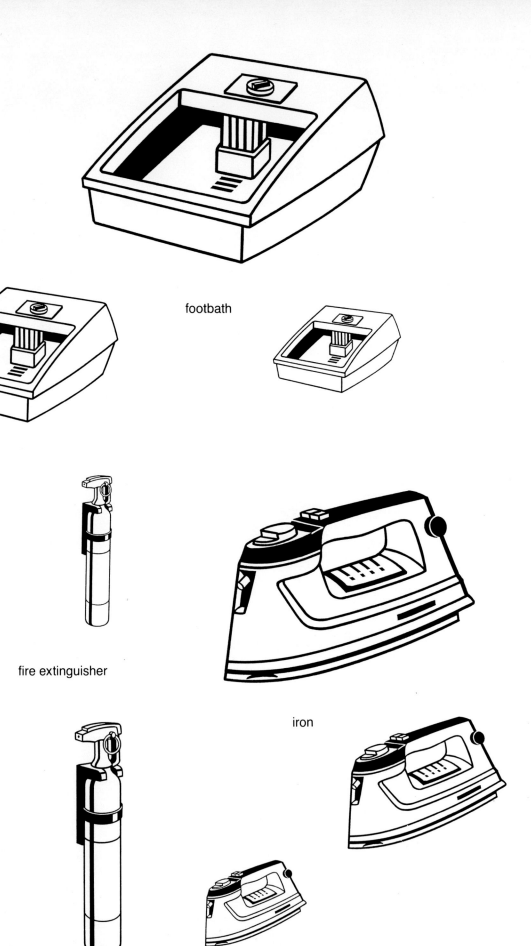

footbath

fire extinguisher

iron